INTRODUCTION

Continuing the 'Vintage Steam Album Series' we come to the magnificent Showmans locomotives. These engines are sure eye catchers wherever they attend, providing as they do a very colourful spectacle with their gleaming paintwork and shining brasswork.

We are fortunate that a considerable number of these fine locomotives have survived into preservation. Those which are featured in this book have all worked for showmen. Some started life as a road locomotive being purchased and converted to showmans engines, while many were supplied new to amusement caterers.

Over the preservation years a number of traction engines have been converted to showmans specifications, while many visitors to a rally would not appreciate any differences, none are included here, these engines will be covered in a future title, together with the showmans tractors which have also received the same treatment.

By far the largest number of 'showmans' in preservation were built by Burrells of Thetford, Norfolk, their engines being especially well liked by Showman. Other famous builders such as John Fowler & Co. (Leeds) Ltd. are represented by various designs, one of the oldest survivors being number 9393 'Sir John Fowler', an engine which spent it's early days on furniture haulage before being purchased by a showman. Among the most recent are examples of the B6 'Super Lion' design, extremely powerful road engines capable of hauling very heavy loads. Fosters of Lincoln also built a large number of showmans locomotives. here again a well respected company with products highly regarded by the travelling showman.

Three other companies are represented by sole survivors, Aveling & Porter by the massive 8NHP 'Samson', an engine which was built in 1901 for the Admiralty and later passed into showland use when the traditional fittings were added. Fodens of Sandbach, Cheshire also built a small number of showman engines, unfortunately, only one survives, this being number 2104 'Prospector', built in 1910 which is now preserved, together with several other showmans engines, of various makes, all are preserved in the same county that the Foden showmans was built. This fine engine attends a number of rallies each year, often accompanied by another sole survivor from the same collection the McLaren 10 NHP 'Goliath', here again an engine which was originally used on gun haulage work for the War Department before being purchased for use on the fairgrounds. Finally, of the sole survivors the Brown & May number 8742 'General Buller' is to be seen at many events, being preserved in the County of Lincolnshire. The company Brown & May were at Devizes in Wiltshire, other than the showmans the remaining engines which the company built are all portables with one exception.

In their working days the showmans engines always attracted engine enthusiasts. Usually well maintained they were very much in the public eye with their coloured lights and shining metalwork. The major fairs would have a number of engines providing power for a whole variety of rides. When it was time for the fair to move, the showmans engines would move off each heading several wagons, the major showman owning several engines. The engine crews were 'masters of their art' negotiating narrow entrances, difficult and often narrow twisting, hilly roads. The engines making a fine spectacle as they encountered any gradients on route.

Showmen also used tractors for the lighter loads, these will be featured in a forthcoming title 'Showmans Tractors', while for the many followers of the road locomotives another separate title 'Road Locomotives' will feature these engines including such famous designs as the Fowler B6 'Super Lions' which worked for Norman Box, handling in their working days some really mammoth loads. As mentioned earlier the various showmans conversion will not be forgotten, as they are of course, very much part of todays rally scene, these will appear in a title later in the series, which when completed will provide full coverage of the steam engines now to be seen at rallies.

Included in the picture selection are some engines rarely seen on the rally field, while others have become exhibits now rarely, if at all, seen in steam, while others have left for preservation abroad.

Meanwhile, enjoy this selection of magnificent Showmans Road Locomotives, now fortunately preserved by dedicated enthusiasts for all to enjoy, all made possible by modern engineering techniques, thus keeping these giants of a bygone age in working order as a fitting tribute to British engineering.

With a background of the 'Giant Wheel' two Burrell showmans road locomotives, 'Lord Nelson' on the left and 'Majestic' await another busy day. 'Lord Nelson' is works number 3443 of 1913, Majestic is number 3890 of 1922. 'Lord Nelson' is part of the Beaulieu Museum collection.

1. 'Samson', Aveling & Porter type LC8 showmans road locomotive number 4885 was built in 1901, being supplied new to The Admiralty and used at H M Dockyard, Chatham. It was converted to a showmans engine for Charles Presland, ending its working days on threshing duties.

2. Only one showmans engine built by the Devizes, Wiltshire company Brown and May, survives. 'General Buller' is a 6NHP engine built as works number 8742 in 1912. When new 'General Buller' was supplied to J. Cooke of North Wales travelling the fairgrounds with a set of gallopers. The engine later changed hands and was owned by Hibble & Mellors of Nottingham. The engine is seen here in fine condition having undergone a major overhaul.

3. This veteran Burrell, works number 2072, dates back to 1898, 'The Masterpiece' was supplied new to John Cole of Yate, Bristol, working for many years with a set of three abreast gallopers. The engine was later to pass into the ownership of another Bristol showman, Messrs. Hardiman & Strong. The rear wheels of this engine are not rubbered which is in keeping with showmans engines of this period.

4. On the left of this photograph is 'Endurance', a 8NHP Burrell built in 1903 as works number 2547, spending many of its early years on haulage work. In 1933 it came into the hands of showman Maurice Stokes of Basingstoke and was converted to full showmans specification, original fittings coming from Burrells. When photographed this engine was awaiting a complete overhaul and its return to the rally scene when fully restored is eagerly awaited. On the right is the unique Brown & May showman 'General Buller'.

5. Burrell works number 2668 'Britannia' was built in 1904. This 8NHP engine was supplied to William Thurston of Cambridge, later being owned by Stanley Thurston and finally J H. Manning of Stevenage, Herts.

6. 'Black Prince', an archive photograph taken in 1963. This Burrell, number 2701 was built in 1904, working in its showland days for Fred Gray, Hampstead, London. This engine is now part of the famous Bressingham collection. Note the flywheel brake.

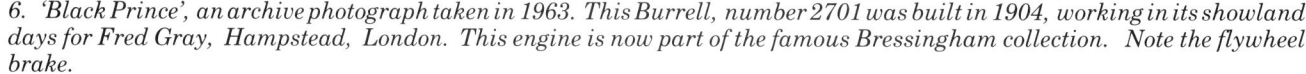

7. 'The Griffin', Burrell 2804 built in 1906 was supplied new to Alf. Payne of York, when she was named 'The White Rose of York', the engine later passed through several showland owners including Anderton & Rowland, Bristol, Charles Heal & son, Glastonbury, Somerset, R. Wilson, Sunbury, Middlesex. finally ending with Pat Collins of Bloxwich, Staffordshire, where it was renamed 'The Griffin'.

8. Burrell 7NHP design 'Princess Royal' was supplied new to Henry Thurston and carried the name 'Lord Nelson', later passing into the ownership of F. Harris & Sons, Ashington, Sussex, when it was named 'Sweet Nothing' and subsequently 'Princess Royal'. The engine is works number 2879 being built in 1907.

9. The Burrell 'Fermoy' was built in 1909 as works number 3090. The engine was supplied new to Pool & Bosco showmen of Birmingham, in 1921 it was purchased by Mrs. Shepherd, another amusement caterer in the Birmingham area. In 1927 the engine changed hands again, this time going into agricultural work.

10. Burrell 3090 'Fermoy' again, this time showing the flywheel side. The engine is a 6NHP design having left the Burrell works at Thetford in 1909.

11. 'Dreadnought', Burrell 3093 of 1909, this engine spent the whole of its working life with the Holland family, going new to Arthur Holland of Swadlincote. The engine is fitted with a crane tower on the bunker, this modification was done at Burrell's works.

12. Burrell works number 3118 'Dreadnought' was built Thetford in 1909 going new to William Cross of Workington, it was later sold to East Anglian amusement caterers C.W. Abott of Norwich, spending many years on the East Anglian fairgrounds hauling and providing power for a Cake Walk and a set of Chair o' Planes.

13. Number 3334 'The Baillie' was built by Burrells in 1911 and is an example of their 8NHP design. The engine was supplied new to George Green of Glasgow, later it was owned by another Glasgow showman H. Bradley, finally ending with Silcock Bros. of Warrington, Lancashire.

14. Burrell 6NHP showmans locomotive 'Princess Mary' (a popular engine name). This one is works number 3343 built in 1911, the engine started its working life as a road locomotive returning to Thetford in 1921 and being fully converted to showman specification, being sold to Herbert Stocks of Ipswich, Suffolk, working for them until the start of the Second World War.

15. Over the years Anderton & Rowland of Bristol owned eleven Burrell showmans road locomotives, five being supplied new, including this one, works number 3443 'Lord Nelson' which was built in 1913. This engine is in preservation at Beaulieu Museum.

16. Burrell number 3444 'His Lordship' was a familiar sight on fairgrounds in Scotland and the North of England. The engine is a 8NHP design built at Thetford in 1913, going new to Green Bros. of Glasgow and later to Green Bros. of Preston, Lancashire. In 1932 the engine was sold to Mr. Edward Silcock of Warrington and used by this owner up until 1950.

17. 'Perseverance II' is a Burrell 3483, a 8NHP scenic engine built in 1913. The engine was supplied new to Messrs. Harniess Bros. of Swinton, Yorkshire. In 1944 the engine changed hands going to Mrs. J Cole of Chichester, Sussex, who used it for three years, it was sold into preservation in 1953

18. 'King George V1', Burrell number 3489, built in 1913. In showland days it was owned by Swales Bolesworth of Dagenham, Essex, when it was named 'City of London', later going to E. Andrews Jnr. of Tunbridge Wells, Kent where it became 'King George V1'

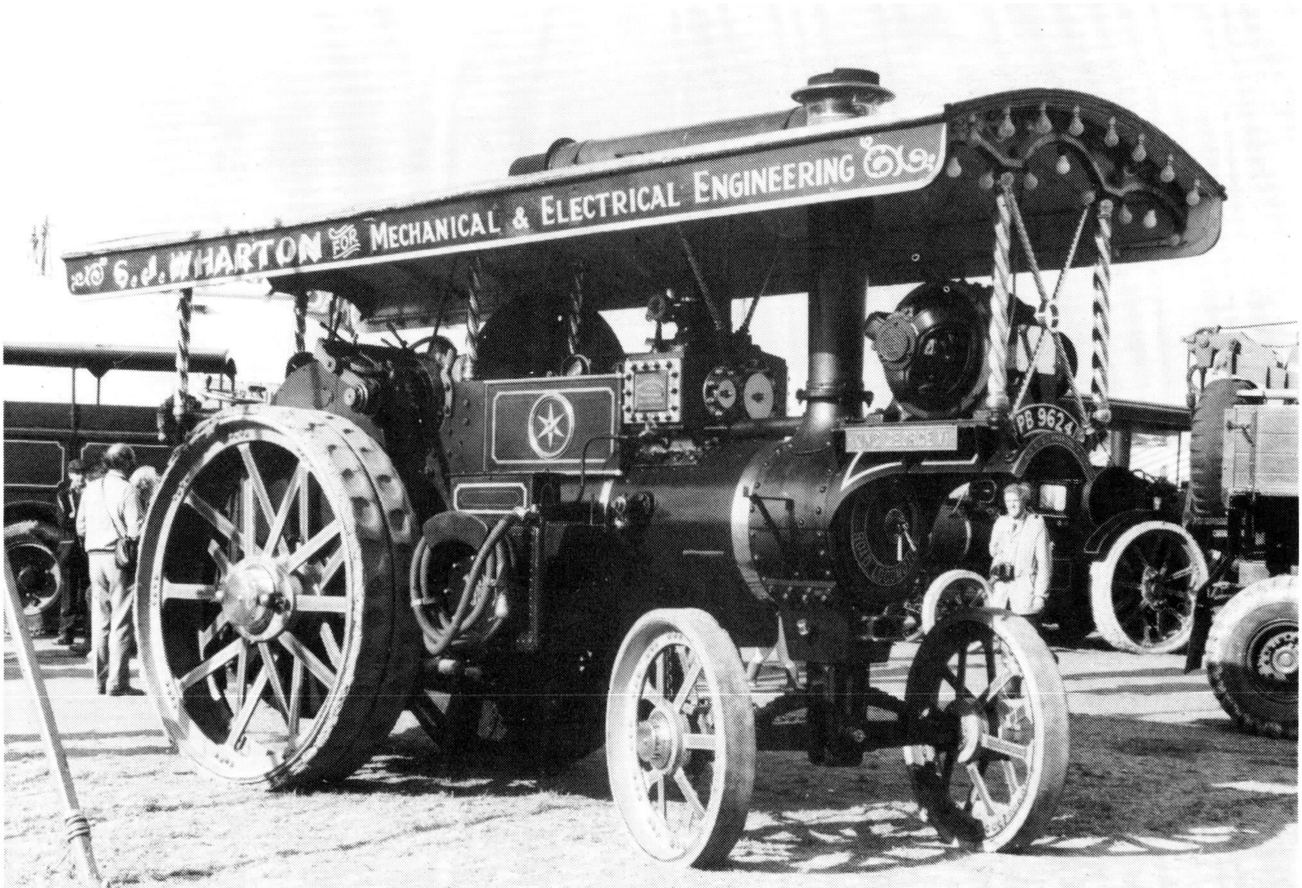

19. 'Lightning 11' was built by Burrells in 1913 and carries their works number 3526. The engine was supplied new to Emerson & Hazard of Whitehaven. This engine was unique in that it was the only showmans engine to leave the works painted green.

20. Burrell 5NHP locomotive number 3555 'The Busy Bee' built at Thetford in 1914 and supplied new to Taylor Brothers, of Workington, Cumberland, touring the fairgrounds of the North of England with a steam driven Switchback. The engine is an example of the 'Devonshire type' and has been in preservation since 1952 when acquired by its present owner. The usual method of stowing the extension chimney on top of the canopy can be seen.

21. Burrell 7NHP showmans engine works number 3651 'Earl Kitchener' was built in 1915 spending its first years on haulage duties. Purchased by R. Edwards & Sons, Swindon Wiltshire in 1920 and converted to a showmans engine travelling with a set of Golden Gallopers.

22. 'Nero' was supplied new to the Travelling Circus Menagerie Proprietors Bostock & Wombwell who were based in Glasgow. This showmans engine must be one of the most widely travelled showmans locomotives, as the menagerie toured the entire country. Burrells completed 'Nero' in 1915 as works number 3669, being an example of their 5NHP design.

23. Burrell 6NHP showmans, works number 3703 'Lady Mary' was built in 1915, the engine was purchased new by Robert Wynn of Newport, Monmouthshire and used on general haulage. Four years later the engine returned to Burrells works and was converted to full showmans specification, going to George Rogers of Chipping Sodbury, Gloucestershire.

24. 'Starlight' was used in it's showland life by R. Edwards & Sons, Swindon, Wiltshire. This Burrell engine is works number 3836, a 6NHP design which was built in 1920. The engine was restored from a very derelict condition and has been seen on the rally field for a great many years.

25. Burrell 6NHP 'Princess Marina' was supplied new to Mrs. Hannah Parkin of Ipswich, the engine subsequently was owned by John Barker & Sons, Ipswich. 'Princess Marina' is works number 3847 and was built at Thetford in 1920.

26. 'No. 1' was built by Burrells in 1920 being a scenic 8NHP design. The works number is 3865, being supplied new to Pat Collins of Bloxwich, Staffordshire.

27. For a number of years 'Island Chief' was preserved in North Norfolk as was the case when the photograph was taken in the early sixties. The engine is a Burrell 6NHP, works number 3878, built in 1921. The first owner was Robert Payne of Hull in whose ownership the engine carried the name 'Excelsior', when sold to Arnold Brothers, Cowes, Isle of Wight the name changed to the present one.

28. For a great many years this fine Burrell 'Island Chief' was missing from the rally scene. This second photograph shows the engine as it was in 1989. 'Island Chief' remained in showland life until 1949.

29. Burrell scenic showmans engine number 3884 'Gladiator' as it was in 1963. This 8NHP engine built in 1921 was new to Fred Gray of Hampstead, London, carrying the name 'Wonder Gladiator'. Scenic engines were fitted with a separate exciter dynamo to the rear of the chimney which provided the field excitation for the main generator. Heavy rides were much easier to start using this method of control.

30. Scenic showman number 3886 was built by Burrells of Thetford in 1921. 'Lord Lascelles' was supplied new to Harry Gray of Battersea, London. A fine example of Burrells 8NHP scenic design.

Plate 1. Fowler B6 'Super Lion' showmans locomotive Supreme was built in 1934 for a Welsh Amusement Caterer and was in fact the last showmans engine built by Fowlers of Leeds. This engine was supplied with left hand steering and chrome fittings in place of the usual brass. Some of the last work that this engine performed was hauling railway locomotives to Glasgow docks.

Plate 2. 'Samson' is the sole surviving Aveling & Porter S R L. This type LC8 engine was built in 1901 for the Admiralty and used at Chatham Docks. It was later converted to a showmans locomotive for Charles Presland, after its showland service 'Samson' ended it's working days threshing, until purchased for preservation.

Plate 3. 'Admiral Beatty' was originally built as a road locomotive and converted to a showmans locomotive in 1921 for Henry Thurston, travelling the East Anglian Fair Grounds. The engine is works number 14153 and was built in 1916, it is a 7NHP double crank compound.

Plate 4. 'Carry On' was built by Fowlers of Leeds in 1915 being commandeered by the War Department for gun haulage in France during the First World War. It was converted to showmans specification in 1923 and sold to Cadonas of Glasgow. In 1943 the engine was sold to McGiverns in Northern Ireland, this engine was the last showmans in everyday use retiring in 1959. The engine was purchased for preservation in 1961. 'Carry On' was photographed while attending a 1978 rally.

Plate 5. Burrell S R L 'Earl Haig' travelled the West Country and London areas while owned by a Gloucestershire showman. The engine is number 3979, a 7NHP, 3 speed, DCC, built in 1924. This photograph was taken in 1974.

Plate 6. 'Princess Mary' was built by Burrells of Thetford in 1922 as works number 3933, the engine is a 7NHP, DCC, 3 speed engine and was built for John Anderton of Exeter, travelling throughout the West Country.

Plate 7. A very rare engine. 'General Buller' was built by Brown and May of Devizes. Wiltshire, in 1916 as works number 8742 being the only surviving showmans locomotive built by this company. The engine was built to the order of a North Wales Amusement Caterer, ending its showland days working in Nottinghamshire.

Plate 8. Burrell 'Scenic' showmans road locomotive 3912 'Dragon' was built in 1921 for the West Country showman Anderton and Rowland, who operated a number of engines, many of which were Burrells. This engine is a 8NHP, DCC, 3 speed design.

31. Burrell 'Scenic' number 3887 'Prince of Wales' was built in 1922 and supplied to Henry Jennings & Son of Devizes, Wiltshire, hauling and powering their Whales Scenic ride. An engine well known in the West Country during its working days.

32. Burrell 8NHP 'Scenic' works number 3888 'General Gough' was built in 1921 and supplied new to S. Bolesworth & Son of Dagenham, London. Like so many fine engines it ended up derelict, in this case in a disused gravel pit.

33. 'Majestic' a fine example of the Burrell 7NHP design built in 1921 as works number 3890. This engine was supplied new to Messrs. J H Herbert of Southampton, who owned the engine until 1952. From the start of the Second World War, this engine was laid up until sold in 1952.

34. Burrell number 3909, a scenic engine built in 1922 and supplied new to A. Holland of Swadlincote, carrying the name 'Pride of the Road', the engine has since been renamed 'Winston Churchill'

35. Anderton & Rowland of Bristol purchased five Burrell showmans road locomotives new. This one, number 3912 'Dragon' being the last purchased in 1921. The engine is a 8NHP 'Scenic'. 'Dragon' was also owned by another Bristol showman. Note the extra brasswork on this engine; swaged brass boiler bands, stars etc. 'Dragon' has smaller rear wheels, a distinct advantage on the West Country hills.

36. Henry Thurston & Sons of Northampton purchased this fine Burrell number 3926 new in 1922. The engine is a 5NHP design which was named 'Margaret'. When new the engine worked a new set of Chair O' Planes and later a scenic railway. This engine is preserved in Holland and now carries the name 'Stokomolief'.

37. Three Burrell showman road locomotives carry the name 'Princess Mary', this one is preserved in Norfolk. The engine left the Thetford works for John Anderton of Exeter, Devon. It was later in the ownership of G A Whittle & Sons, Woking, Surrey. 'Princess Mary' is works number 3933, a 7NHP engine built in 1922.

38. Burrell scenic 3938 'Quo Vadis' was built in 1922 and supplied new to William Wilson of Peckham, London, for use with his 'Rodeo Dragon Car Switchback', remaining in the same ownership until 1940 when it was sold to Walls Brothers of Petersfield, Hampshire who operated the engine until 1955. 'Quo Vadis' is now in Ireland.

39. 'Princess Mary', this Burrell was the last to appear on a British Fairground while owned by a showman, this being in 1958. 'Princess Mary' is works number 3949 and was built in 1923 going new to Billy Nichols of Forest Gate, London, it was later owned by Charles Presland of Tilbury, Essex. This engine has a lower canopy covering an wider radius, this was a feature from new and required in view of low bridges that the engine had to negotiate on its travels.

40. 'Earl Haig' Burrell 3979, a 7NHP design built in 1924 for Mrs. F. Symonds of Gloucester. Throughout the engines working life it travelled in the West Country, with the very occasional visit to the London area.

41. Burrell 10NHP scenic showmans road locomotive works number 4000 'Ex Mayor'. Supplied new in 1925 to G. T. Tuby & Sons of Doncaster, Yorkshire. The name 'Ex Mayor' originates from Mr. Tuby's civic position in Doncaster. This superb Burrell attends events in many parts of the country.

42. Burrell 'Scenic' showmans 'Dolphin', a 8NHP engine being the last Thetford built showmans engine, supplied new to William Davies of Stoke on Trent, Staffordshire. In the late twenties it was sold to John Shaw a Sheffield based showman, and later moving to H J Wallis of Seaforth, Lancashire. 'Dolphin' is works number 4030 being built in 1925. The engine was originally 'Dolphin' but during its showland days has also carried the names 'The Guvnor' and 'The Commando'.

43. The last surviving Foden showmans road locomotive is number 2104 'Prospector', built at Sandbach, Cheshire in 1910. The engine was supplied new to W. Shaw & Sons of Sheffield, travelling the Yorkshire fairgrounds for a great many years. Fodens only built ten showmans road locomotives.

44. This Foster, number 14153 'Admiral Beatty' was built in 1916 as a road locomotive. In 1921 it was converted for use as a showmans engine for Henry Thurston. travelling the East Anglian Fairgrounds.

45. Foster showmans engine 'The Leader' was built at Lincoln as works number 14446 in 1921, being supplied new to Pat Collins, remaining in service until 1958. 'The Leader' was the last showmans engine to appear at Nottingham Goose Fair in 1957.

46. Foster 7NHP 'Victorious' was built at Lincoln in 1920 for T. Pettigrove, Stonebridge Park, Middlesex. The engine, works number is 14501. While in showland service the engine travelled extensively in the London area.

47. 'Victory' is another fine example of Foster showmans road locomotives. Number 14502 is the sister engine to 'Victorious', both leaving the works on the same day. This engine was new to Mrs. C Bird of Watford, Hertfordshire and used in the London area fairgrounds.

48. 'Success', Fosters built this powerful 10NHP showmans road locomotive in 1932, it being supplied new to Hibble & Mellor, Nottingham, travelling in the Midlands. The works number of this engine is 14632.

49. Fowler 9393 'Sir John Fowler' started life as a road locomotive on haulage works in the Somerset area. In 1921 it was purchased and used by Anderton & Rowlands of Bristol. The engine did not carry twisted brasswork on the roof supports. In 1926 the engine changed hands again, going to Jim Noyce who used the engine until 1941. This Fowler is a R1 class design, built in 1905, and is one of the oldest Fowlers to survive.

50. Fowler B class, 14425 'Carry On' was built in 1916, and was like so many engines, taken over by the War office for gun haulage in France. In 1923 the engine was converted to showmans specification and sold to Cadonas of Scotland, in 1943 the engine was sold to McGiverns of Northern Ireland, from whom it was purchased for preservation.

51. Fowler number 15117 'Headway' was built at Leeds in 1920 and supplied new to Hibble & Mellor in Nottingham. This fine engine is a class R3 of 8NHP and weighing thirteen tons.

52. Fowler 8NHP showmans 'Repulse', a R3 class design. This engine was built to special order of John Murphy of Gateshead, County Durham, the engine travelling for many years with their Proud Scene Peacock ride. The works number of 'Repulse' is 15652.

53. The other engine used with Murphys 'Proud Scenic Peacock Ride' was 'Renown', like 'Repulse' built to special order from Fowlers being works number 15653. This engine is fitted with a Thompson - Watson Feast crane used for lifting parts of the ride.

54. 'Renown' again, this side showing the other side of the engine, the feast crane mentioned previously can be seen at the rear of this engine's canopy. Note this Fowler carries no twisted brasswork, hence the words on the front of the canopy 'Plain but Powerful'.

55. Fowler 7NHP showmans number 15657 'The Iron Maiden' was built in 1920 and supplied new to Portland Stove Quarries, Dorset. It was later converted to full showmans specification. In it's showland life it was owned by Mrs. H Oadley of Derbyshire. In its working days the engine carried the name 'Kitchener'.

56. Another photograph of the flywheel side of the 'Iron Maiden', an engine known to many having been seen on Cinema and Television screens starring in a film of that name. The engine is a R3 class design.

57, Fowler B6 'Super Lion' design, works number 19783 'King Carnival II', this fine showmans locomotive was built at Leeds in 1932 and supplied new to F. McConville at West Hartlepool, Co. Durham, travelling extensively in the North of England. The engine was used during the Second World War for heavy haulage ending its working days at John Thompson Boiler Makers at Wolverhampton being sold for preservation in 1951.

58. 'Supreme' The last showmans locomotive built by Fowlers, being completed in 1934. This engine was built to special order with left hand steering and chrome fittings replacing the usual brass. 'Supreme' was supplied to Mrs. A Deakin & Sons, Brecon, remaining in showland use until the Second World War, when the engine was used for heavy haulage in Glasgow. The works number of this engine is 20223, being a B6 'Super Lion' design.

59. Another sole survivor is McLaren showmans road locomotive 'Goliath', a 10NHP engine which was supplied to the War office in 1917 for haulage of heavy guns in France. After hostilities ceased many engines were offered for sale. 'Goliath' was purchased by Pat Collins of Walsall and converted to full showmans specification. The works number of this Leeds built engine is 1623.

60. Another view of McLaren 'Goliath', a magnificent engine which weighs twenty five tons, with rear wheels that are 9' 6" overall. This engine has been fully overhauled in recent years.

61. An interesting archive shot taken in 1963 shows Burrell 3093 'Dreadnought'. The 8NHP design engine which left the Thetford works in 1909 for Arthur Holland of Swadlincote. This engine is now preserved in Cheshire with several other showman locomotives.

62. Another photograph of the Fowler B6 'Super Lion' number 19783 'King Carnival II', taken in 1980. This engine spent its last working years on heavy haulage for John Thompson Boiler Makers of Wolverhampton and was used by them until purchased for preservation in 1968.